HUMAN DEVELOPMENT:
THE WORLD AFTER COPENHAGEN

by

Richard Jolly

The 1996 John W. Holmes Memorial Lecture

Reports and Papers
1997 No. 2

ACUNS
Brown University, Box 1983
Providence, RI 02912-1983

Telephone: 401/863-1274
Fax: 401/863-3808
E-Mail: ACUNS@brown.edu
Internet: http://www.brown.edu/Departments/ACUNS

Thomas G. Weiss, Ph.D., Executive Director
Melissa Phillips, Program Coordinator
Janet Kalunian, Program Assistant
Kevin W. Dahl, Staff Assistant

Reports and Papers are published and distributed by the Academic Council on the United Nations System as part of its program to expand the understanding of the problems of international cooperation and the role of international institutions. The individual author(s), however, remain responsible for the content of the work that is presented.

©1997 by the Academic Council on the United Nations System. All rights reserved under International and Pan American Conventions. No part of this report may be reproduced by any other means, electronic or mechanical, including photocopy, recording, or any information storage and retrieval system, without prior written permission from the publisher. All inquiries should be addressed to the Academic Council on the United Nations System.

ISBN 1-880660-12-1

TABLE OF CONTENTS

About the John W. Holmes   i
Memorial Lecture Series

About the Author   ii

Human Development: The World After Copenhagen

Human Development—An Idea Whose Time Has Come	1
Human Development and Economic Growth, 1960-1994	6
The Role of the UN in Following Up on the Global Conferences	12
A Focus for Future International Development Assistance	16
Collaboration with the Bretton Woods Organizations	21
Donor Support	23
The Broader Challenge	24
Notes	26

Recent Publications   inside back cover

ABOUT THE JOHN W. HOLMES
MEMORIAL LECTURE SERIES

The Academic Council on the United Nations System inaugurated the John W. Holmes Memorial Lecture Series in 1989 in honor of a founding member of ACUNS. Mr. Holmes had served on the planning committee for the founding conference of ACUNS and the provisional committee in 1987-88. The talk he prepared for the first ACUNS annual meeting in 1988, *Looking Backwards and Forwards*, was the first publication in the Council's series of Reports and Papers.

John W. Holmes joined the Canadian Department of External Affairs in 1943 and participated in the planning of the United Nations. He attended the preparatory commission in 1945 and the first session of the General Assembly, and later served as head of UN Affairs in Ottawa and as Under-Secretary of the Department of External Affairs. In 1960, he left public service for a second career in teaching and scholarship, basing himself at the Canadian Institute of International Affairs and the University of Toronto.

Mr. Holmes brought to the Academic Council a lifetime of experience and reflection on international politics and the role of the United Nations. He also brought a marvelous mix of idealism and realism, a mix that showed up clearly in the report, *Looking Backwards and Forwards*. In the conclusion, he spoke of the need for reexamining the role of the UN in a way that captures the basic purposes of the Academic Council. "It is an ideal time," he said, "to launch in all our countries that renewed examination of past experience of the UN, to discover on what we can build and where not to venture, how we can use the growing threat to the globe itself to create the will for international self-discipline which is what international institutions are all about."

About the Author

*R*ichard Jolly is special adviser to the administrator of the United Nations Development Programme (UNDP) and architecht of the *Human Development Report*. He was previously director of the Institute of Development Studies at the University of Sussex before joining the United Nations Children's Fund (UNICEF) as deputy executive director for fourteen years. He is co-editor of *Adjustment with a Human Face* and *The Bretton Woods Institutions and the United Nations: Challenges for the Twenty-First Century*.

HUMAN DEVELOPMENT: THE WORLD AFTER COPENHAGEN

Richard Jolly

John W. Holmes' talk for the first annual meeting of the Academic Council on the United Nations System (ACUNS) in 1988 was titled *Looking Backwards and Forwards*. I would like to put the emphasis in this article on looking forwards—from Copenhagen plus one to the year 2000, 2015, or even 2030. In short, I would like to direct attention to the world that the United Nations will need to face in the years ahead, and explore how human advance can be carried forward over that period, rather than dwell on the predicaments in which the world is at present caught up or through which the UN has struggled over the fifty years of its existence.

HUMAN DEVELOPMENT—AN IDEA WHOSE TIME HAS COME

A plethora of pledges, declarations, and reports on human development has underscored the importance of human development over the last five years and has taken it as a central theme and priority. The succession of goals and commitments of the global conferences of the 1990s has helped sharpen this focus and give it legitimacy.

The first of these, the World Summit for Children, focused on children and recognized that the "achievement of child related goals in the areas of health, nutrition, education, etc. . ." would require the "revitalization of economic growth and social development in the developing countries" (along with actions) "to address together the problem of abject poverty and hunger that continue to afflict too many people in the world." The "children's summit," however, did not actually use the phrase "human development"—nor did the World Bank's important report on poverty issued in June that same year. However, two years later, at the Earth Summit in Rio, the phrase "human development" began to creep into the argot and, by 1994, at the Cairo International Conference on Population and Development (ICPD), it was a common phrase for what a few years earlier had been referred to as social development, investment in human resources, human–centered strategy, advancing the human condition, and the like.

It was the World Summit for Social Development in Copenhagen, in March 1995, where this notion of human development was most clearly enthroned. The summit's declaration reads, "We will create a framework for action to place people at the center of development and direct our economies to meet human development needs more effectively."[1]

Many individuals, governments, UN agencies, and nongovernmental organizations (NGOs) played a part in mobilizing attention and commitment to this goal of human development. Tribute must be paid to Ambassador Juan Somavia of Chile, who conceived the idea of the summit and demonstrated the energy and diplomatic skills to make it happen. And the Danish government deserves praise not only for hosting the meeting and providing a large part of the resources but for resisting the voices of caution urging, "Not another conference!" Tribute, I believe, should also be paid to Jim Grant, the former executive director of the United Nations Children's Fund (UNICEF), who five years earlier had organized the first summit on a human development theme—children—and who afterward visualized how the UN could mobilize global action to achieve basic goals for children in a hundred or more countries, thereby providing an important part of the inspiration for the Copenhagen meeting. I recognize these individuals and specific governments to make the point that vision and leadership are critical ingredients of successful international action—yet components too often ignored or underestimated, whether in accounting for success (or failure!) or devising a plan for reform.

Much of the intellectual credit for the entrenchment of the idea of human development must go to Mahbub ul Haq, architect and creator of the United Nations Development Programme's (UNDP) *Human Development Report,* first launched in 1990. This document not only made a major impact by introducing and establishing the language of human development but, more significantly, gave conceptual clarity and new content to the idea of human development. Human development was defined as a process of enlarging people's choices. The most critical of these wide ranging choices are to live a long and healthy life, to be educated, and to have access to resources needed for a decent standard of living. Additional choices include political freedom, guaranteed human rights, and personal respect."[2]

Later *Human Development Reports* identified three essential components at the heart of the concept:

- equality of opportunity for all people in society. Poverty reduction and an equitable distribution of income are integral to human development strategy;

- sustainability of such opportunities from one generation to the next; and

- empowerment of people so that they participate in—and benefit from—development processes.

The *1995 Human Development Report*, issued shortly before the Women's Conference in Beijing, introduced some additional conceptual breakthroughs by explicitly incorporating gender into both the concepts and measurements of human development. Two new measures were introduced: the Gender Development Index (GDI) and the Gender Empowerment Measure (GEM). The report analyzed many aspects for strategy and concluded that human development, if not engendered, is endangered. These basic points are important to underline at the beginning because human development is often confused with earlier related but ultimately narrower and less fundamental concepts, such as:

- *human resources development,* which emphasizes human *resources* as a critical input, for an enterprise or a whole economy;

- *social sector development,* which is part of the means required to strengthen human development but, ultimately, is a means rather than an end;

- *poverty reduction,* which, though again important, is clearly only part of the larger goal.

In short, human development is a broad and fundamental concept. Human development is the end not a means. Indeed the *Human Development Report* argues that people should be the aim and objective of all development.

It seems not at all surprising that it was UNDP rather than one of the Bretton Woods institutions that gave birth to the ideas of human development and to the *Human Development Report*. The UN has always been more sensitive to pioneering perspectives, more multidisciplinary, less rigorous by the standards of orthodox economics and finance but precisely because of this, more imaginative, more innovative and, ultimately, perhaps, more influential.

The concepts underpinning human development have deep philosophical roots. Aristotle declared, "Wealth is evidently not the good we are seeking, for it is merely useful and for the sake of something else." Immanuel Kant said "So act as to treat humanity . . . in every case as an end, never as a means only." And the great Bengali poet and Nobel laureate Rabindranath Tagore wrote, "We have for over a century been dragged by the prosperous West behind its chariot, choked by the dust, deafened by the noise, humbled by our own helplessness and overwhelmed by the speed. We agreed to acknowledge that this chariot-drive was progress, and the progress was civilization If we ever ventured to ask, 'progress towards what, and progress for whom,' it was considered to be peculiarly and ridiculously oriental to entertain such ideas about the absoluteness of progress. Of late, a voice has come to us to take count not only of the scientific perfection of the chariot but of the depth of the ditches lying in its path."[3]

Human Development and Economic Growth, 1960–1994

So much for the concepts. What about reality? Here the perspectives begin to differ more sharply with the conventional ways of assessing development. Notwithstanding the forthright declarations of the world summits and global conferences, economic and financial orthodoxy still reigns. So measures of inflation, deficits, and economic growth remain center stage, while indices of human development remain to the side—which is unfortunate, as measures of human development in many respects show more impressive advance than measures of economic growth.

Diagrams Ia and Ib show the patterns of economic growth and the advance in human development since 1960. In all countries, human development increases, sometimes faster and sometimes slower, but only in extreme circumstances with an actual decline (as in the Ukraine and in many other Commonwealth of Independent States (CIS) countries, with the desperate collapses of the early 1990s). In contrast, economic growth in many countries shows great fluctuations.

Diagram II shows the great contrasts between levels of per capita income and levels of human development. Many countries with broadly similar levels of human development have achieved this goal with very different levels of income. And pairs of countries with broadly similar levels of per capita income, such as Ecuador and Morocco, Tunisia and Namibia, Venezuela and South Africa, and Malaysia and Iraq, differ widely in their rates of literacy, life expectancy, and child mortality.

DIAGRAM IA

TRENDS IN HUMAN DEVELOPMENT AND ECONOMIC GROWTH BY REGION, 1960-1993

Growth in regional incomes—stunning advance and dismal decline
Real GDP per capita (index, 1960=100)

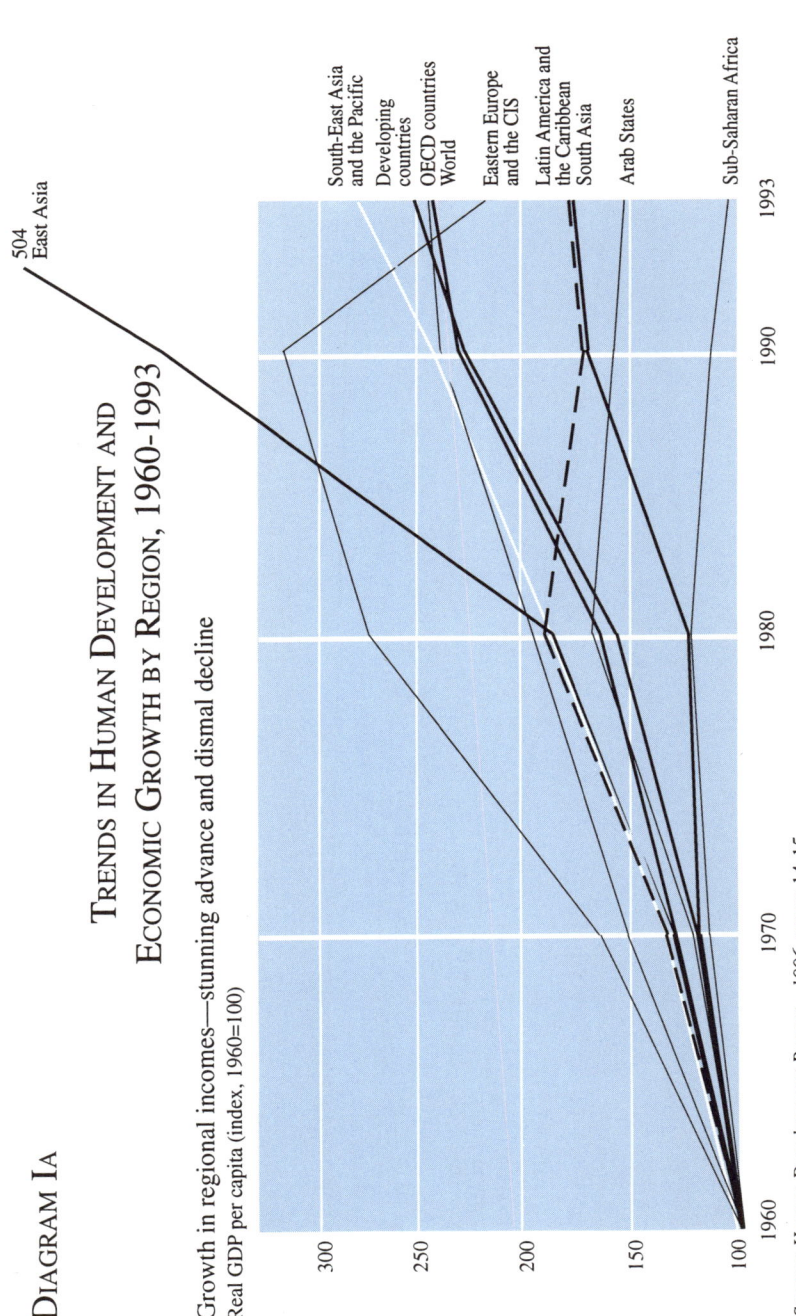

Source: *Human Development Report - 1996*, pages 14-15.

DIAGRAM 1B

TRENDS IN HUMAN DEVELOPMENT AND
ECONOMIC GROWTH BY REGION, 1960-1993

Human development has improved steadily in most regions—but faster in some than in others

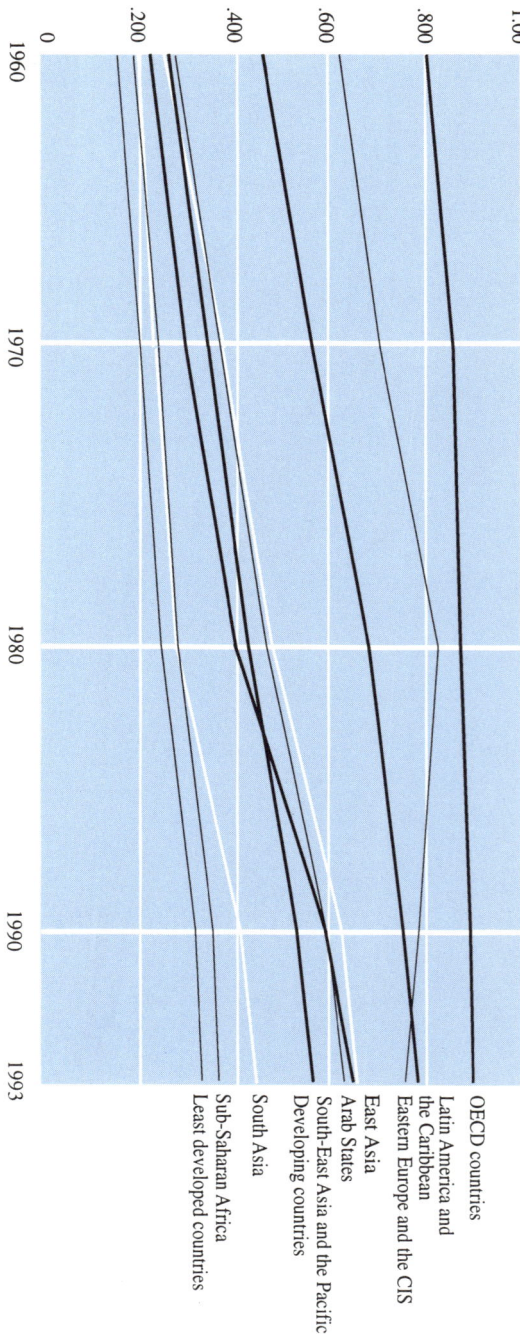

Source: *Human Development Report - 1996*, pages 14-15.

Diagram II

Contrasts Between Levels of Human Development and Levels of Per Capita Income

Similar income, different human development, 1993

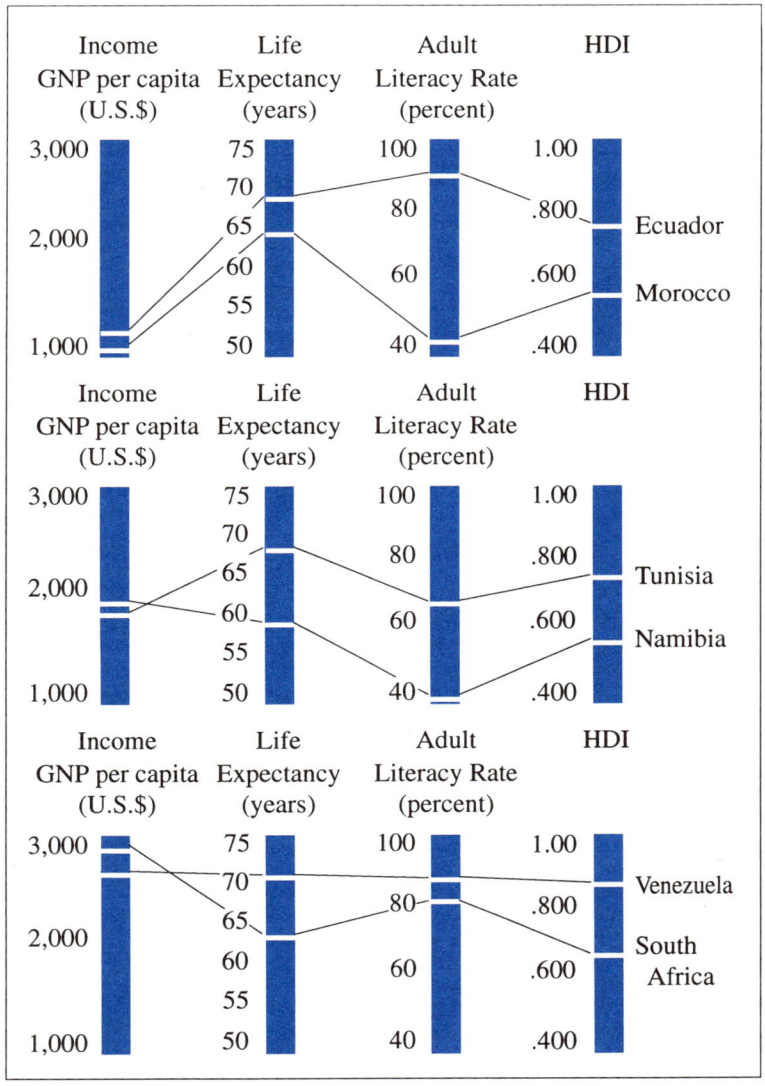

Source: *Human Development Report - 1996*, page 30.

All of this makes clear that economic growth is less central than is usually emphasized. But economic growth is still important, as a *means* to development. Indeed, the latest analysis by the *Human Development Report* Office suggests that, over the medium term, economic growth is important to sustain advances in human development. Although, for a decade or so, human development can advance without economic growth, unless growth catches up, advances in human development tend to slow. Lop-sided growth cannot be sustained. Similarly, in countries like Pakistan, Brazil, and Egypt, which have for a period experienced rapid economic growth, this very growth tends to falter after a period, in the absence of a supporting structure of human development.[4]

Against this background, where does the world stand in the mid–1990s, on the eve of the next century and, indeed, the eve of the next millennium? There are some points of optimism. The vast bulk of countries in the world has shown impressive advances in human development. Over the last few decades, life expectancy in the developing world as a whole has increased substantially (from forty-six to sixty-two years), infant mortality has more than halved (from 150 to seventy), the proportion of underweight children has fallen by a third, the proportion of people with access to clean water has almost doubled (from forty to nearly seventy percent), and average incomes have increased by about three times. Food production and consumption have increased at a rate of about twenty percent faster than population growth, while fertility rates have fallen— more than halfway from where they were in the 1960s to where they must be to attain the conditions required for long-run population stability. By historical standards, these are remarkable and unprecedented advances, more than was ever expected in the postwar years and faster than anything experienced during the first phases of the industrial revolution in the now–industrial countries.

In contrast to the considerable success in human development, the economic record over the last fifteen years has shown serious signs of setback and lack of sustainability. The *Human Development Report 1996* shows that income per capita and average purchasing power in some one hundred countries was lower in 1994 than in the 1980s.[5] In seventy of these countries, it is lower than it was in the 1970s, and for some thirty-five countries, lower than in the 1960s—thirty-five or more years before. All of this represents a most serious setback for the lives of 1.5 billion people, including hundreds of millions in the poorest countries of the world. Economic growth does not guarantee improvements for the poor. But the poor rarely escape the impact of *declines* in per capita income, and often are hit hardest by them.

Notwithstanding these terrible economic setbacks for hundreds of millions of people, I believe that the degree of development pessimism in much of the West today is vastly exaggerated. Indicators of human development have improved almost universally—and usually at unprecedented rates. And, in spite of the setbacks for a third of the world's population, the other two–thirds of the population in developing countries are living in countries experiencing extremely rapid rates of economic growth. These are important points for optimism, especially since the most economically successful countries have shown that it is both possible and desirable to combine human development and poverty reduction with a drive for economic growth. China, Malaysia, Indonesia, and Thailand must now be added to the earlier cases of Korea, Hong Kong, and Singapore as countries where rapid growth has both contributed to and been enhanced by human development and rapid reductions in poverty. Moreover, the latest analyses suggest that a major part of the success of these countries is the manner in which an early emphasis was given to education for all and to equality of opportunity—often with considerable equality of incomes.

THE ROLE OF THE UN IN FOLLOWING UP ON THE GLOBAL CONFERENCES

The global conferences of the last five years have provided a starting point for a major global effort in advancing human development, especially in the countries that have so far been lagging or deficient in the effort. These conferences have, for the most part, set goals, defined a broad plan of action, and provided the basis on which specific country–by–country action can proceed.

There is obviously a risk that the plethora of conferences and the diversity of goals will overwhelm any attempt at focus and follow–up. This can be avoided if the emphasis is clearly put on international support for National Programs of Action (NPAS). Indeed, some 150 countries have already prepared NPAS for follow–up to one or more of the international conferences. Though some of these NPAS lack focus and are weak or deficient in comprehensive costings, they provide an important starting point, especially for setting priorities for poverty reduction and sustainable human development.

Experience in the process of follow-up to the World Conference for Children (and to related conferences such as the Talloires meeting, which set health goals for the year 2000, and the Jomtien conference on Education for All) has already demonstrated how a small core of international goals adapted through NPAS can provide the priorities for international action and partnership. Even within five years, tangible results and remarkable success have been demonstrated in scores of countries and in all regions of the world. There is already clear evidence of major reductions in child mortality, increases in primary education, and dramatic reductions in the prevalence of polio, guinea worm, tetanus, iodine, and vitamin–A deficiency, toward the eventual goals of eradication.[6]

These advances have often involved strong actions by the governments concerned, at regional, district, and municipal levels as well as by central governments. District– and municipal–level programs of action have been prepared in more than fifty countries. Often, this has been part of a process of national mobilization involving the media, religious groups, NGOs, and much of civil society in ways that have made implementation of these goals a widespread national effort. Collaborative support by the international community has also often been important, especially to support and accelerate national action. International support has come from the main UN agencies (UNDP, UNICEF, the United Nations Population Fund (UNFPA), the World Health Organization (WHO), the United Nations Educational, Scientific and Cultural Organization (UNESCO), and the

World Bank), many of the bilateral agencies and international NGOs, and religious groups and others such as the Rotarians and the Scouts.

No doubt, there can be many interpretations of what have been the critical ingredients of this success, in ensuring that the goals for children agreed on at international conferences have been carried forward into successful, widespread action in more than a hundred countries. Drawing on my own experience in UNICEF, UNDP, and the collaborative bodies of the UN system, I identify five essential elements in explaining the success:

1. Strong international leadership and commitment to follow–up and to "make a difference." In this case, one must identify, in particular, the personal role of Jim Grant, the executive director of UNICEF from 1980-1994. He showed how the head of a UN agency can reach far beyond the UN in articulating the need for action on a worldwide scale and then in helping to mobilize a grand alliance to achieve it.

2. The clear commitments of one of the main UN agencies with field offices—in this case UNICEF— to focus on and support national action toward the goals, and work at the country level to help mobilize broader partnerships of technical and financial support for their implementation. The critical requirement is for such an agency to have the commitment, the field presence, and the financial resources to act as a lead agency, in the sense of accepting the responsibility that "the buck stops here": that is, if something is going

wrong, and if international support is proving inadequate, the lead agency must have the commitment, the resources, and the determination to do everything it can to make it right.

3. Strong and widespread support from the other concerned UN agencies, including WHO, UNESCO, UNFPA, and UNDP—and, often, with much financial support and a different form of partnership with the World Bank.

4. Focused support in many individual countries and, internationally, from bilateral donors and international NGOs.

5. Country–level monitoring, generated by the country itself and backed up by monitoring through the offices of the main UN agencies. There have been frequent regional and global reviews to assess the results, together with periodic reports to the executive boards of the agencies and to ECOSOC. Especially important has been the public dissemination of country-by-country performance through publications such as the *Progress of Nations*. Such publications have a wide media outreach and have consciously played up an element of competition amid country-by-country comparative performance.

In setting out these elements, I have drawn directly on UNICEF experience. But I firmly believe that the positive lessons of this experience are much more widely applicable—and could do much to offset the sense of failure and lethargy in some parts of the international community at this time.

A FOCUS FOR FUTURE INTERNATIONAL
DEVELOPMENT ASSISTANCE

How might this approach be used to provide a focus for development assistance in the future? The starting point is to regain momentum—by setting out a vision for the next stage of international development, and building on recent assessments, goals, and perspectives of the recent international conferences. A beginning on this has already been made in recent months. Four main interagency task forces have already been set up within the UN, focused on coordination between the agencies in four main areas of action:

- basic social services for all (chaired by UNFPA)

- full employment and sustainable livelihoods (chaired by the International Labour Organization [ILO])

- enabling environment for people-centered sustainable development (chaired by the World Bank)

- empowerment and the advancement of women.

The first of these grew out of the interagency task force established by UNFPA to mobilize follow-up within the UN to the ICPD held in 1995.

The ICPD task force demonstrated again the importance of five critical elements for effective follow-up: committed and charismatic leadership; clear focus on country-level action; concentration on a few priority actions linked to both the global and the national plans of action in the country concerned; recommendations of the program of action for priority attention; and a common advocacy framework. A further important task of follow-up action has been the establishment of a working group to identify and agree on a common core of indicators.

As supercoordinator for the whole process is the administrator of the UNDP. At an earlier point in the history of the UN, the director-general would probably have been chosen. In my view, there is a strong rationale for the UNDP administrator to hold this position, primarily because this individual is directly in charge of the resident representatives and UNDP field offices. The director-general, for all his/her earlier eminence as second in command to the secretary-general, never had field troops to command. Yet such staff and resources are needed, even though responsibility for implementation must always be with the government, the private sector, NGOs, and other groups within the country concerned. The advocacy, support, and monitoring role of the UN agencies is usually critical.

How effective will be the new process of follow-up remains to be seen. If it is to be effective, it will be necessary for the boards and administrations of the key UN funds and specialized agencies to establish a strong commitment and culture of follow-up, reinforced by a number of basic priority actions:

- The UN agencies, in their respective boards, will need to agree that a major part—say, half to three–quarters—of their country efforts and resources will be devoted to the support of country–level actions toward goals agreed in the global conferences.

- Stronger collaboration is needed with the UN at the country level in support of these goals and efforts. The Country Strategy Notes, recently created, should be used to sharpen the interagency focus on support for national goals of poverty reduction, human development, and sustainability. The UN resident coordinator should give a clear lead in these efforts, supported by the UNDP administrator, both in his roles as "supercoordinator" for the secretary-general and as UNDP administrator.

- As part of the resident-coordinator system, a team approach to program support should be used in the key areas of priority action. A number of countries already have experience in this, bringing together the concerned UN agencies (sometimes with interested donors) in such areas as rural development, education, and child and reproductive health care. The teams are usually chaired by one of the agencies most directly involved, but all work under the overall team leadership of the resident coordinator. This approach helps to build up genuine collaboration, but without blurring the basic lines of responsibility and accountability. Using the goals for focus, such teams should now be established in all countries where the government is willing and interested.

- The consultative group and roundtable meetings for countries and donors should increasingly be brought into this process, making progress toward the goals a key point for review at each meeting. Such review should also include consideration of donor and agency support for the goals and the extent to which resources are being allocated for poverty reduction, human development, and sustainability. The 20/20 formula can be used to provide a rough guide for evaluating this status. In time, also, it may be desirable to explore for some of the poorest and least developed countries some form of international compact between the country concerned and a small core of committed donors to assure the country of longer–term support as it accelerates toward such goals as the provision of primary education for all.

- A strong country–by–country monitoring system needs to be made a critical part of the above, to ensure that both within the country and internationally, timely information is available on progress toward the goals and on the course corrections required. The UN agencies including the World Bank can provide support for this monitoring. It will be important that this be established through strengthening national capacity, rather than by building up an independent system focused primarily on international needs. But the international agencies can ensure that national data once generated are properly and professionally evaluated and brought together into some form of international report. Such a report needs to be regularly issued, publicly available, and frank and objective in assessing progress and international performance while providing support for national efforts.

A simple illustration of how the interagency support for these efforts might look at the country level is set out in Diagram III. This identifies the crucial leadership role of the resident coordinators and the UNDP, the critical

DIAGRAM III

ACTION PRIORITIES AND MAIN UN INVOLVEMENT
IN POVERTY REDUCTION

Goal	Action Priorities	Main UN Operating Agencies Involved
	A. Macro Strategy	UNDP, but with other agencies, interacting with World Bank and IMF
	B. Income Generation for Poorest	
	• access to productive assets (credit, inputs, land)	UNDP, UNIFEM, and IFAD, with FAO, ILO
Poverty Reduction	• Household food security	FAO, IFAD, WFP
	C. Basic Social Services for All	
	• primary health care (including reproductive health), basic education, nutrition, water, sanitation	UNICEF, UNFPA, with WHO, UNESCO
	D. Monitoring	UNDP, UNICEF, UNFPA with FAO, WHO, ILO, UNESCO, and UNSO

role of the other funding agencies in their main areas of action, and the supportive roles of the various specialized agencies.

COLLABORATION WITH THE BRETTON WOODS ORGANIZATIONS

My own belief is that we should neither expect nor seek to establish total uniformity of approach between the international financial institutions and the rest of the UN agencies. Their focus, approach, mandates, and voting systems differ—inevitably creating occasions when policies and attitudes in particular situations also differ.

The World Bank and the International Monetary Fund (IMF) have been the dominant influence on the macroeconomic policies of most of the poorest and least developed countries over the last decade or so—and, increasingly, also the dominant influence on donor coordination. The very dominance of this role has often attracted criticism, together with criticism of some of the economic policies that have been promoted in this way. In recording this observation, it is important also to recognize the changes made to some of these policies in recent years, especially by the World Bank, in giving much more serious attention to poverty reduction and to the social sectors.

Recently, the World Bank has moved to a more open and flexible policy of collaboration with other UN agencies, just as several of the UN agencies have moved to closer collaboration with the World Bank. There is, however, some way still to go to establish more effective and pragmatic relationships in which the experience and approaches of the UN agencies can influence the Bank and the IMF, and vice versa. In fact, UN agencies such as UNDP, UNFPA, and UNICEF have rich areas of experience, as well as different approaches. They also have a comparative advantage that could be of benefit to the Bretton Woods institutions, based on their strong field presence and on their smaller–scale and lower–cost operations, both of which are important for cost-effective action on poverty. Moreover, relationships between the UN agencies and governments are often less one-sided and more partnership–oriented than are those with the Bretton Woods institutions. All of this could be of advantage in establishing closer working relationships between these actors.

On matters of macro policy, the IMF and the World Bank clearly will continue to have the dominant voice—though I hope it is increasingly recognized that other agencies can often make a helpful contribution by their different perspectives and more detailed knowledge of particulars related to poverty reduction, human development, and sustainability. Ways should be found for the Bretton Woods organizations to draw more on this expertise, especially at the country level. The UN agencies often also have useful field–level experience of low–cost, interdisciplinary, and more participatory approaches which, if drawn on, could help the whole international effort achieve greater efficiency, effectiveness, and sustainability. The UN system has generally also been more closely involved with implementation of the goals arising from recent international conferences.

Donor Support

All of this is made easier because of the recent agreement of donor governments who participated in the high-level meeting of the Development Assistance Committee (DAC) of the Organisation for Economic Cooperation and Development (OECD) to give a priority focus to support of a vision for the twenty-first century, with three goals in priority areas of action:

1. Economic Well-Being

    - a reduction by one-half in the proportion of people living in extreme poverty by the year 2015.

2. Social Development

    - universal primary education in all countries by the year 2015.

    - demonstrated progress toward gender equality and the empowerment of women by eliminating gender disparity in primary and secondary education by the year 2005.

    - a reduction by two-thirds in the mortality rates for infants and children under age five and a reduction by three-fourths in maternal mortality, all by the year 2015.

    - access through the primary health-care system to reproductive health services for all individuals of appropriate ages as soon as possible, and no later than the year 2015.

3. Environmental Sustainability and Regeneration

- preparation of national strategies for sustainable development in all countries by the year 2005, so as to ensure that current trends in the loss of environmental resources are effectively reversed at both global and national levels by the year 2015.

In their cooperation with developing countries, donor governments have indicated their priority interest in support of national actions toward these goals. As part of these efforts to define a clearer focus, regional meetings could be held over the next year or two to strengthen a climate of partnership and commitment as well as to identify more specific points that would help implementation and greater efficiency.

THE BROADER CHALLENGE

The achievement of these goals no later than the year 2015—and, in some countries, perhaps much earlier—would represent a real advance in laying the foundation for sustainable human development over the next century. But it will not be enough to focus only on poverty eradication—or even on support for the poorest and least developed countries.

As emphasized before, over the last fifteen years some one hundred countries have experienced unsustained economic growth, often for a decade or more. Incomes fell precipitously or faltered so long that, even today, standards of living and levels of income in many of these countries are below levels reached many years earlier. In forty or so countries, for instance, levels of income are lower than they were more than twenty-five years ago. It is totally insufficient and misleading to say that the cause is simply the individual failure of each of these countries to adjust efficiently to the new world of the global–market economy. Near simultaneous failure in a hundred countries is evidence of something more systemic.

Moreover, global inequality has been rising. The gaps in income between the richest twenty percent of the world's population and the poorest twenty percent have doubled from thirty to one in 1960 and sixty to one in the early 1990s. The poorest twenty percent of the world's people have seen their share of global income fall from 2.3 to 1.4 percent, while the share of the richest twenty percent has risen from seventy to eighty-five percent.

The forces that have given rise to these trends—and allowed them to continue with so little remedial action in such critical areas of policy as debt trade, technology, and aid—need much greater international attention and stronger and more sustained global policy. The UN has, over the whole of its fifty years, often demonstrated both awareness of such global issues and intellectual creativity in analyzing them and in suggesting solutions. In this respect, the UN record is more successful than is often acknowledged. Sometimes the solutions proposed have been adopted—as with International Development Assistance (IDA), Official Development Assistance (ODA), and some of the environmental actions agreed at the Earth Summit in Rio and earlier. Others have proved to be too far in advance of their time, in terms of political acceptability or technical feasibility—as with many of the UNCTAD proposals for fairer trade and technological relationships, or the measures to assist least–developed countries. Awareness of global imbalance and creative action to deal with its most glaring manifestations now needs to be transformed into a new focus for international partnerships between the UN and the Bretton Woods organizations (including the new World Trade Organization [WTO]). Agreement will not be easy or rapid, but agreement and action are essential if the next phase of global development is to be put on a track of diminishing inequality, greater balance, and greater sustainability for the world as a whole—and especially for the world's poorest countries and poorest people.

NOTES

1 *Copenhagen Declaration*, World Summit for Social Development, Copenhagen, March 1995.

2 Ibid., p. 1.

3 Quotations in UNDP *Human Development Report 1996* (Oxford, New York) 1996, p. 45.

4 See *Human Development Report 1996*, Chapter 3.

5 Ibid, p. 3.

6 A full report on progress at mid-decade toward the goals for the year 2000, agreed at the World Summit for Children, has been prepared by UNICEF and was submitted by the Secretary-General to the General Assembly.